PETER'S JOURNEY

Text copyright © 2020 by Karen Gray Ruelle and
Deborah Durland DeSaix

Illustrations copyright © 2020 by Deborah Durland DeSaix

All Rights Reserved

HOLIDAY HOUSE is registered in the U.S. Patent and Trademark Office.

Printed and bound in November 2019 at Tien Wah Press, Johor Bahru, Johor, Malaysia.

The artwork was created with graphite and watercolor.

www.holidayhouse.com

First Edition

1 3 5 7 9 10 8 6 4 2

Library of Congress Cataloging-in-Publication Data

Names: DeSaix, Deborah Durland. | Ruelle, Karen Gray.
DeSaix, Deborah Durland.

Title: Peter's war / written by Deborah Durland DeSaix & Karen Gray Ruelle ;
illustrated by Deborah Durland DeSaix.

Description: 1st ed. | Audience: Ages 6–10.

Identifiers: LCCN 2012006580 | ISBN 9780823424160 (hbk.)

Subjects: LCSH: Feigl, Peter, 1929– | Jewish children in the
Holocaust—Juvenile literature. | World War, 1939–1945—
Children—Europe—Biography—Juvenile literature.
Jewish children—Europe—Biography—Juvenile literature.
Holocaust, Jewish (1939–1945)—Biography—Juvenile literature.

Classification: LCC D804.48 .D48 2020 | DDC 940.53/18092—dc23

LC record available at https://lccn.loc.gov/2012006580

ISBN: 978-0-8234-2416-0 (hardcover)

To KAREN GRAY RUELLE — D.D.D.
To DEBORAH DURLAND DeSAIX — K.G.R.

Peter, age three, in 1932.

PETER was born lucky. His parents adored and pampered him. At a time when many people were out of work, his father was a successful businessman in Berlin, Germany. Peter's family had servants, took vacations at the seashore, and lived a life of luxury.

Then in 1933, just three years after he was born, Peter's luck changed: Adolf Hitler was appointed chancellor of Germany. By 1934 Hitler had proclaimed himself the *Führer*—the supreme leader of Germany—and gained complete power there.

Hitler promised to restore Germany's glory and put Germans back to work. World War I had thrown Germany's economy into chaos, but Hitler blamed the Jewish people for all of Germany's problems. Many Germans were already anti-Semitic—prejudiced against Jews—and believed he was right. Hitler's Nazi government immediately began passing laws against Jews.

When Peter was young, he had no idea that he was Jewish. Although his parents were of Jewish descent, they never took him to synagogue or observed Jewish holidays. The family celebrated Christmas along with other Germans. In spite of all that, in the eyes of the Nazis they were Jews.

In 1939 German troops invaded Poland, igniting World War II. Hitler intended to conquer Europe and murder all the Jews. Peter and his parents spent years running and hiding as the Nazis took over one country after another.

When Peter was thirteen, he was separated from his parents. He fought to survive as the war escalated around him. This is his story.

Adolf Hitler saluting troops at a parade in Nuremberg, Germany.

Vienna, 1938: The sign on the park bench means "Only for Aryans!" Nazis believed that Germanic people were the superior race, Aryan, and that Jews, even German Jews, were not Aryan. So, while dogs were allowed to sit on this bench, it was forbidden to Jews.

Vienna, 1938: Austrian Nazis try to humiliate Jewish men by forcing them to scrub the pavement by hand.

From the very beginning of Hitler's rise to power, Peter's parents tried desperately to keep their son safe from the Nazis. They even took him to a Catholic church and baptized him to hide his Jewish roots. They moved from Germany to Czechoslovakia, and then to Vienna, Austria, but no matter where he lived, the boys at school bullied Peter and called him a Jew. He was angry. Why were they calling him a Jew? He was a Catholic!

One morning Peter awoke to a changed world. Overnight, the Nazis had covered Vienna in red and black banners triumphantly displaying the swastika—the symbol of their power. They had taken over Austria.

Ein Volk, ein Reich, ein Führer! The words reverberated in Vienna's Town Hall Square. The words meant "One people, one empire, one leader!" All around Peter, thousands of people chanted their support for Hitler, and Peter was swept up in the frenzy, shouting until he was hoarse. Drums pounded and horns blared. At long last, Hitler began to speak. The crowd was mesmerized.

Later, Peter's mother found out where he had been. She roared, "Don't you ever call that monster *our* Führer! He's our enemy!" and she slapped him hard.

Peter's parents knew that they would have to move again. His father hoped they would be safer in Belgium, but Jews were no longer allowed to move out of Nazi territory. They'd have to pretend they were just going on a short vacation. Peter was upset when he had to leave all his toys behind and take only an overnight bag on the train.

At the Belgian border the train was stopped, and inspectors searched every piece of luggage. Peter could tell that his mother was terrified. Finally, they let the train move on.

The Vienna Boys' Choir gives the Nazi salute, welcoming Hitler to Austria in March 1938. The banner reads "We sing for Adolf Hitler!"

Peter's family found an apartment in Brussels, Belgium. His grandmother joined them, and for two years they all felt safe. But then, on a spring day in 1940, the Nazi army rampaged across Holland and surged into Belgium. The police arrested Peter's father and took him away. Peter, his mother, and his grandmother fled to France on foot, hitching rides when they could.

A flood of people was rushing south toward France. Nazi planes swooped over the road, strafing everything in their path, even hitting cows in the surrounding fields. Peter dove for cover along with everyone else. The night they reached Paris, an air-raid siren began to wail—the Nazis were closing in. They scrambled onto an overcrowded train heading south, out of the city. An official told them they would find help at Oloron-Sainte-Marie, but it was a trick. When they got there, men with machine guns forced them into the back of a truck and drove them away.

Peter, his mother, and his grandmother were imprisoned in the most dreadful place they'd ever seen: Gurs, an internment camp for refugees, political prisoners, and Jews. It was crowded and filthy. Peter was always hungry and he was itchy with lice. Rats ran through the barracks where he slept.

The Gurs internment camp.

Within weeks the Nazis defeated France, and a Nazi inspector arrived at the camp. Peter's mother marched right up to him and said, "Heil Hitler! I am a German citizen and I demand that we be released instantly from this stinking hole!" The astonished Nazi called them a taxi and let all three of them go.

They settled in the town of Auch, where they waited for his father to be released. Meanwhile Peter's grandmother left for America. Finally, Peter's father was temporarily released from a prison camp because he was very ill. When he joined them in Auch, Peter was thrilled, but he constantly worried that his father might be sent back.

Peter in Auch, France, in June 1941.

Peter and his parents in their backyard in Auch, France, in April 1942.

They were very poor, and Peter's parents felt trapped in France, but at least they were together again. Over the next two years, they tried to get by. They dreamed of escaping to America.

In the summer of 1942, Peter overheard his parents whispering. There were rumors of mass arrests of Jews. They were put on trains heading east, out of France, and none of them ever came back.

Peter's parents sent him away to a summer camp in a town called Condom. One day, his father bicycled all the way there to see him. He gave Peter a pouch made from a handkerchief, and told him to keep it safe. It contained the only valuables his parents had left. When his father rode away, Peter burst into tears, overwhelmed with fear that he would never see him again.

A few days later, Peter found out that his parents had been arrested, and no one knew where they had been taken. He was devastated.

He tore out the used pages from his notebook, and he wrote:

This diary is dedicated to my parents in the hope
that it will find them both alive and well.
Their son, Pierre Feigl, Condom, August 27, 1942

The first two pages of Peter's diary. The writing on the
left-hand page says, "This diary is dedicated to my parents
in the hope that it will find them both alive and well.
Their son, Pierre Feigl, Condom, August 27, 1942."

The postman came. I ran to ask whether there was anything
for me. Thank God.——A postcard from you; you're in the Vernet
internment camp. . . . I'm pleased; and hope that they'll let you
go because of Papa's poor health. —from Peter's diary

Peter waited. Every day he hoped to hear from his parents. He was sure he would see them soon, and he wrote to them faithfully in his diary.

At last two postcards arrived from his mother, but only one was for Peter. In the other, his mother begged the camp director to take care of her son. Peter believed his parents would be released and would come to get him, but instead an official letter was delivered, saying that they had been sent to a transit camp. One more postcard arrived for Peter, but after that, nothing.

Then the police came for Peter. They already had his parents, but they had orders to arrest Peter too. They showed up three times, but every time, the camp director tricked them, pretending that Peter was very ill and couldn't be moved.

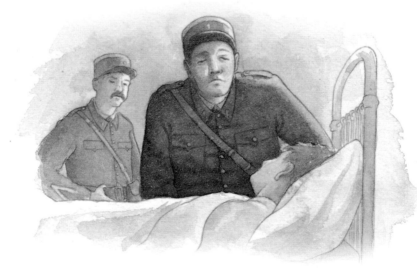

Thursday [September] 3
I'm anxious. Madame C. [the camp director] got a letter with
my Baptismal certificate and 3 ration cards for shoes and
nothing else. . . . I'm worried. I'm afraid that you're gone.
I'm still in bed [sick]. I'm afraid for you, my good parents.

Saturday [September] 12
. . . I cried tonight. Who knows where
they're taking you?

The camp director knew she had to send Peter away to keep him safe, so she found a place for him on a ship for Jewish children, bound for safety in America. He had to wait until the ship was ready, so he stayed at a children's home on the outskirts of Marseille. There was never quite enough food, but he liked it there anyway. He made friends and explored the city—and he kept his diary, always telling his parents how much he missed them.

Then, just two weeks before the ship was scheduled to sail, the Nazi army closed the port and no ships were allowed to leave. Peter was trapped in France.

Peter discovered that Nazis had taken over a farm across from the children's home. That gave him an idea. He spoke German. What if he were to wander over and talk to them? Maybe they would share their food with him. So he tried it. The Nazis liked Peter, and for a few days, he ate very well.

Then, one day, the Nazi captain became suspicious. He asked Peter what on earth a German boy was doing in Marseille. Peter thought fast, and told him that he was spying on his classmates for his father, who was in the Gestapo—the Nazi secret police.

Peter got away with his scheme until the director of the children's home found out what he was doing. The director was furious, and said that he was recklessly putting them all in danger.

On the last day of 1942, Peter pasted photos of his parents into his diary. He missed them terribly. He was bored and restless, and Marseille was becoming very dangerous. The police were constantly stopping people on the street and demanding their identity papers, and there were rumors that the Nazis were preparing to arrest all the Jews in the city.

In early January he was sent to a children's home in Le Chambon-sur-Lignon, a tiny village up in the mountains. His train arrived on a bitterly cold night, and then he had to walk miles through the snow to get there.

Peter was happy in Le Chambon, but he still missed his parents. He continued to write to them in his diary. His last entry was made on January 31, 1943: *Another month has gone by and I still haven't heard from you.*

On February 1, when Peter looked for his diary, it was gone.

Peter's diary, showing the page where he pasted the photos of his parents. At the beginning of 1943, he switched from writing in French to writing in German.

Peter, studying with other boys at Les Grillons, the children's home in Le Chambon, France, where he lived. He is in the center, smiling at the camera.

The terrace of La Maison des Roches, where some young refugees were sheltered in Le Chambon. The Gestapo arrested eighteen of them in June 1943, along with the director. He was also in charge of Les Grillons, the children's home where Peter lived.

Le Chambon was filled with young Jewish refugees like Peter. Jews, and anyone in France caught sheltering them, could be arrested and killed at any time. Early one June morning, the Gestapo stormed into Le Chambon, hunting for Jews. They arrested some young men, as well as the director of Peter's home, and took them all away. Peter's home in Le Chambon was no longer safe.

Soon after, someone came to take photos of Peter and all his friends, to make false identity papers. Many of Peter's friends would be guided to Switzerland, a neutral country that was not involved in the war. Peter's French was practically perfect, so he could hide elsewhere in France under his new identity, Pierre Fesson.

Before they left Le Chambon, Peter and his friends exchanged photos, signing each one. "To a sweetie, Pierrot [Peter's nickname], from a friend who likes you, Odette." "To my friend Pierrot, in memory of your friend Antonio." "To my oldest friend, who always makes me mad!" "To my love, Rosario, from her admiring Peter."

Peter kept all the photos of his friends as mementos. He kept two from Rosario.

Peter was sent west to a boarding school in the town of Figeac. He was very lonely there, and he worried that people might think he was Jewish, so he went to church every Sunday and pretended to pray.

On New Year's Day, 1944, he started a new diary. In it, he boasted about his studies and agonized over his problems with other students and teachers. He also noted every plane that passed overhead and every air raid in Figeac, and began making cryptic entries about the escalating Nazi activity around him.

Some of Peter's friends in Le Chambon, France. Rosario is second from the left, top row.

Even though he was only fourteen, Peter fought the Nazis by helping the Maquis—a network of French Resistance fighters. They found out that he spoke German, and asked him to translate some stolen German documents for them. He also eavesdropped on the Nazis in town and reported their conversations back to the Maquis. He sabotaged Nazi trucks, and even went along with the Maquis when they blew up a Nazi factory nearby.

Frequent air raids sent everyone in Figeac running for cover. One day the streets filled with Nazis and their tanks, and Peter could hear the staccato of machine-gun fire as he sat in study hall. The Nazis ordered every male in Figeac between the ages of sixteen and fifty-four to report to the police station. From there, the Nazis would take them away.

Peter wasn't taking any chances. He clambered up onto the school's roof and slid over to the adjoining church. He hid in the bell tower and watched the Nazis rounding up all the men. He stayed there until morning, waiting until the Nazis had left town with their prisoners.

Then the Maquis picked up rumors that the Germans had figured out that someone in the school was reporting on them. They decided that Peter had better get out of there. Arrangements were made for Peter to go to Switzerland, but he would have to sneak across the border. His real identity papers were hidden in the lining of his jacket. He stashed his diary at the bottom of his backpack, and traveled by train to a town near the border. He was warned to pretend not to know the other refugees who were also making the trip.

Peter drew a map of his border crossing in his diary that day. The writing is in French: *Suisse* means Switzerland; *barbelés* means barbed wire; *forêt* means forest; *porte* means door or gate; *jardin* means garden; *route* means road; and *vignes* means vineyard. Sorral II is the name of the place on the Swiss border where he crossed.

When they got off the train, they followed *passeurs*—people smugglers—across a field, over railroad tracks, and into the woods. It was cold and rainy, and a young child was crying. After a long while, Peter realized that they had passed the same spot three times—they were lost. Finally, the *passeurs* found what they were looking for, and pointed through the trees to a barbed-wire fence. They told everyone to lie down on the wet ground—they had to wait for the right moment to cross the border. Peter was soaking wet, and he was freezing.

Suddenly the *passeurs* signaled, and everyone leaped up and rushed for the border fence. Peter threw his backpack over the barbed wire and slid underneath. He sprinted toward a second fence, and scrambled through it, onto Swiss soil.

He was safe. Peter's war was finally over.

Monday 22 [May 1944—the day Peter crosses the border into Switzerland] [The Swiss] welcome us. The interrogation (the first) begins already. I get out my real [identity] papers, which were sewn into my jacket. Around 1 p.m. a truck came to get us. It took us to Geneva to the Claparède camp. Everyone waves to us as we drive by. There [at the camp], the questioning begins. We eat well. At 7 p.m. I take a shower and they inspect our heads [for lice]. Then I sleep well in a free land. —from Peter's second diary

EPILOGUE

Peter's war ended when he arrived safely in Switzerland, but it was not the end of his journey. He was lucky not to have been sent right back over the border to France, as some refugees were. He spent two years in Switzerland, bouncing from home to home, a troubled, angry young man who couldn't settle down. During this time, he gradually sold most of the things in the packet his father had given him in Condom. Then he found out that his aunt and grandmother were in the United States. They sponsored him to join them there.

Peter was seventeen when he arrived in New York in 1946. He spoke almost no English, and carried with him the same backpack he had brought from France. He also had his second diary, fifty-eight photos of his friends from Le Chambon, and seven dollars in his pocket.

His relatives urged him to go to school, but Peter wanted to get a job, to be independent, and to earn enough money to go out on dates. He found work quickly, but as soon as he turned eighteen he joined the Air Force. He had dreamed of becoming a pilot since he was a little boy.

However, because he was not a U.S. citizen, Peter wasn't allowed to become a pilot, so he trained instead as a translator for technical intelligence. He went on to a very successful career in international aviation. The high point of his career was serving at a top post in the Department of International Security Affairs at the Pentagon.

Peter's wife, Lennie, died in 2018. She was also a Jewish refugee from Germany. He has two children and two grandchildren.

In 1950 Peter learned from the International Red Cross that his parents had been sent to Auschwitz, a Nazi death camp in Poland created for the sole purpose of killing Jews. It wasn't until 1991 that he saw an actual list of people sent to Auschwitz, and found his parents' names there. They had been sent to their deaths in early September 1942, only a few days after their arrest. He realized that for nearly the entire time he had been writing to them in his diaries, they were already dead—murdered by the Nazis.

Peter and his bride, Lennie, on their wedding day in 1954.

The photo on Peter's Swiss identity card.

Amazingly, Peter's first diary reappeared forty years after the war ended. It was published in France by someone who had found it in a flea market and assumed the author had perished. Then the publisher saw Peter in a documentary about Le Chambon and contacted him. The diary is now in the United States Holocaust Memorial Museum archives in Washington, D.C., along with Peter's second diary, some letters and official wartime documents, and all of his photographs.

Peter's story has been featured in books and documentaries in the United States and overseas, and his diaries are the basis of an educational program created by the USC Shoah Foundation. For many years, he has spoken at schools, libraries, and conferences, describing his experiences during the war and sharing his insights. His resilient and irrepressible spirit continues to inspire everyone he meets.

Peter as a baby in Berlin, 1930.

Peter at age six, 1935.
His father's company sold
Champion sparkplugs.

Peter on a Sunday afternoon outing near
Brussels, with his parents and a friend,
1938 or 1939. Peter is on the right.

Peter in Marseille, autumn 1942.

Young refugees posing in front of Les Grillons, the
children's home where Peter stayed in Le Chambon-
sur-Lignon, in 1943. Peter is seated at the left end
of the front row.

Peter in his family's backyard
in Auch, spring 1942.

NOTES

Peter Feigl recounted many of the stories and personal details in our book during our interviews with him and in his United States Holocaust Memorial Museum oral history. All excerpts from his diaries are either his translations from the original German (from the archives of the United States Holocaust Memorial Museum) or our translations of the original French.

P. 5

Adolf Hitler called his plan to murder Europe's entire Jewish population the Final Solution of the Jewish Question. By 1945, as a result of this hatred, around six million Jews had died in what is known as the Holocaust. *Jews* were defined by the Nazis as anyone with Jewish ancestry, even if they didn't consider themselves Jewish.

Nazi laws against Jews were draconian. Jews couldn't own radios, go to the movies, or shop in non-Jewish stores, and they had to obey strict curfews. Eventually they were barred from owning property and were even kicked out of their own homes. Most jobs were forbidden to Jews, so they had no way of earning money. Many parks, public places, and buses had signs saying No Jews Allowed.

Jews were required to wear a yellow six-pointed star sewn onto their clothing at all times, to identify them as Jews, and they frequently suffered humiliation and beatings when they ventured out. Later, in some places, Jews were forced to live in ghettos, where food was so scarce that many people starved to death.

The Nazis built concentration camps and death camps to carry out their murderous plan. Concentration camps imprisoned innocent people in brutal conditions. Death camps were set up solely to kill large numbers of people. In Auschwitz alone, which was both a concentration camp and a death camp, more than one million Jews—men, women, and children—were killed. During all this time, anyone who tried to help Jews risked being arrested and punished—and possibly being sent to the camps themselves.

PP. 6-7

Peter's family were secular Jews who didn't

practice their faith, and Peter had been baptized as a Catholic. In his USHMM oral history, Peter recounts being punched by other children in Vienna and called a Jew, and he remembers his anger because he was actually Catholic. It was common for Jewish children to be bullied for their religion. In a recent email to the authors, Peter recalls this differently: he has no memory of being bullied as a child for being Jewish.

In 1993, Czechoslovakia peacefully separated into the Czech Republic and Slovakia, two separate countries.

Peter told us that when they were living in Vienna, his mother would go shopping every day and would exchange the traditional Austrian greeting *Grüss Gott!*—God be with you!—with the local grocer. When they discussed politics, the grocer insisted that Austrians would never let Hitler into their country.

On March 12, 1938, the Germans took over Austria in what is known as the *Anschluss*. Peter told us that he remembered his mother bursting into tears the night before, while listening to a speech on the radio. His father was away on business in Switzerland, so it was just Peter and his mother. At school, Peter remembers seeing that Hitler's portrait and red flags with black swastikas had been put up in every classroom. The swastika was an ancient symbol appropriated by the Nazis as the emblem of their regime. When Peter's mother went shopping, the same grocer she met each day now greeted her with the words *Heil Hitler!*—Hail Hitler!—which was the accepted form of greeting in Nazi Germany.

PP. 8–9

Three days after the Nazis took control of Austria, Hitler gave a speech in Vienna's Town Hall Square. Peter was nine years old, and he slipped out of the house to join the enormous crowd. He told us how much he envied the boys in the Hitler Youth as they paraded past in their uniforms. He wished his parents would let him join, so he could wear a Sam Browne belt and a real dagger, like they did.

"Don't you ever call that monster our Führer! He's our enemy!" This is Peter Feigl quoting his mother (his translation from the German); from our interview with him.

Peter told us that a few weeks later, his mother told him to pack his suitcase with some clothes and a few practical items. He would have to leave behind his train set and his beloved blue scooter. Belgium had been neutral in World War I, meaning that it hadn't taken either side in the conflict. Peter's father hoped Belgium would be neutral again if another war erupted.

PP. 10-11

Peter's father took the train every day from Brussels to his job in nearby Antwerp. At school Peter had to learn to speak French and Flemish. Everyone called him Pierre, French for Peter. He joined the Boy Scouts and went to the movies. Peter told us that his favorite film was *Test Pilot*, and that from then on his dream was to become a flier, like Clark Gable in the movie.

The Nazis invaded Poland in September 1939. England and France declared war against Germany, and World War II began. On May 10, 1940, two months after Peter had turned eleven, the Nazi army invaded Holland, Luxembourg, and Belgium. Within a few weeks, all three countries were defeated.

Peter told us that before they fled, his father wanted to go to his office first, to pay his employees. Peter's mother said it was too dangerous, but his father insisted and left for the train station. He didn't come back that night. Several days later, Peter's mother found out that he had been arrested at the station. Because of his German passport, the Belgian police suspected Peter's father of being a Nazi spy! They sent him to a detention camp at a military base near Brussels.

Peter and his mother packed only what they could carry to make the perilous journey south. His grandmother needed a cane to walk, so Peter carried her bag as well as his own. Peter told us that it didn't feel real to him when he saw people dying. He imagined that he was Clark Gable, flying his plane and gunning down the enemy.

Finally, after a journey of more than 150 miles, they reached Paris, where Peter fell into an exhausted sleep in an attic room of his aunt's apartment. When the air-raid siren went off, Peter didn't even wake up, and his mother had to carry him downstairs to the cellar, where everyone in the building huddled in fear. Paris was too dangerous, Peter's mother decided, so they took a train south to Bordeaux.

The officials in Bordeaux told them to take the train to the town of Oloron-Sainte-Marie, where the authorities would help them. It was a nasty trick that would bring them to the town closest to the internment camp of Gurs, where they were then imprisoned.

"Heil Hitler! I am a German citizen and I demand that we be released instantly from this stinking hole!" This is Peter Feigl quoting his mother (his translation from the German); from our interview with him.

Peter told us that the reason his mother was able to fool the Nazi inspector at Gurs was that their passports were not stamped with a big *J* to indicate that they were Jewish. This was because they had gotten their passports before the law requiring this stamp had been passed. She showed the inspector her passport, and he ordered their immediate release. They headed north. When they reached Auch, people warned them that the Germans were just beyond the town, so that's the reason they ended up there.

Peter's father was being held in an internment camp called St. Cyprien, where he was very ill. Finally he was released on a thirty-day convalescent leave. Peter told us that every month, his mother somehow got the leave extended, but they could never be sure that his father would be permitted to stay.

PP. 12–13
The Nazis controlled France, but the country was divided into two parts. The northern half was occupied by the Nazis. The southern half, where Peter's family lived, was ruled by the new French government in the city of Vichy, and was somewhat safer for Jews than the Northern Zone. However, the Vichy officials collaborated with the Nazis, passing many anti-Semitic laws. Vichy police sent thousands of Jews, including babies, to internment camps, to hold them until they could be sent out of the country. The Vichy government was even so cruel as to separate mothers from their children when they were put on cattle cars and sent away to concentration camps or death camps.

Peter's family lived in Auch from 1940 to 1942. They were poor, but Peter's father made some money cleaning old spark plugs. They grew vegetables behind their one-room apartment, kept a chicken, and raised rabbits for the stewpot.

The only route of escape to America at that time

was by ship from Portugal. They each needed four visas: one to leave France, another to enter Spain, another to go from Spain to Portugal, and yet another to enter America.

At one point Peter and his mother had their visas, but they didn't want to leave without his father. When his father's visas came, theirs had already expired, and he wouldn't leave without them.

Peter was thirteen years old in the summer of 1942 when he overheard his parents whispering about mass arrests of Jews. That July, the Paris police arrested around thirteen thousand Jewish men, women, and children, and immediately sent six thousand of them to a transit camp called Drancy. From there they were deported to the concentration and death camps in Germany, Poland, and elsewhere. The rest of those arrested were thrown into the Vélodrome d'Hiver (Vél d'Hiv) sports stadium. The prisoners were held there for nearly a week with little food or water. The few bathrooms quickly became unusable. From there, they were deported to the concentration and death camps, except for a few people who managed to escape. That summer, arrests of Jews escalated, and

the trains taking them to the camps were always full. There were rumors and whispers, but most people in France were unaware of the fate of those who were sent away.

Peter's mother had a job working for a Quaker charity called the American Friends Service Committee, and she arranged with them to send Peter to a children's summer camp at a chateau in Condom. While he was there, he had a surprise visit from his father, who had bicycled twenty-five miles from Auch despite his poor health. He didn't stay long. Peter told us that before his father left, he gave Peter a small bag his mother had sewn from a handkerchief and asked him to keep it safe. Peter described the contents to us: his mother's ring and bracelet, his father's gold pocket watch with a tiny Buddha hanging from the fob, a silver mechanical pencil (a treasure his father had gotten in the United States), a small silver horseshoe, a gold cigarette case, and a miniature spark plug that was his father's good-luck charm. There was also a little money— all that was left of his parents' wealth.

Peter told us that writing to his mother and father in his diary was the only way he could feel close to them after their arrest. He hoped that they would be released soon, but wanted them to know everything he was doing in their absence.

PP. 14–15
The postcards from Peter's mother relayed the bad news that his parents were imprisoned in an internment camp called Le Vernet. Peter's mother implored Madame Cavailhon, the director of the children's camp in Condom, to keep Peter with her as long as she could, and then to ask the Quakers to take care of him. She sent Madame Cavailhon Peter's baptismal certificate and some clothing ration coupons. Within days, word came that Peter's parents had been sent to the Drancy transit camp, the final stop before being sent out of France. The last postcard Peter ever received from his parents was dated just five days after their arrest.

Several days after his parents' arrest, a man from the police station called to warn Madame Cavailhon that Peter was about to be arrested. This man suggested, however, that they wouldn't take Peter if he was too sick to be transported. Madame Cavailhon knew a trick to make it seem as though Peter had a fever. Peter told us that whenever he gives a talk at a school about his wartime experiences, one of the questions he is always asked is "What was the trick?" This is what he tells them: Madame Cavailhon rolled up ten little balls of bread and soaked them in vinegar. She made Peter swallow them whole, one after the other. By the time the police arrived, it had somehow given Peter a burning fever. The policemen took one look at him and proclaimed that he couldn't be moved.

The police came back several times over the next few weeks. Each time, there was a warning, and each time, Peter had a high fever and couldn't be moved. Madame Cavailhon wouldn't let him leave the house without her. Everywhere they went, the police followed them, even when they traveled to Auch to collect his parents' belongings—a trip that lasted from dawn until dark.

The Quaker ship in Marseille had room for about five hundred young Jewish refugees. Peter had to fill out a form in order to qualify for passage, but the Quakers turned him down. He had written on the form that he was Catholic. Madame Cavailhon immediately wrote back, explaining that although he had been baptized Catholic, Vichy still considered him to be Jewish, and his life was at stake.

While they waited, Peter attended Mass every day, praying for the safe return of his parents.

Madame Cavailhon had told him that they would say a novena—nine days of prayer—and then his parents would return. When that failed to work, he was upset.

He wanted to know why God would allow something like this to happen. What had his parents done to deserve it? The priest sent him to the archbishop to answer his questions, but Peter wasn't satisfied with the archbishop's response. He decided that he no longer believed in God, or in any religion.

Madame Cavailhon's letter convinced the Quakers to make room for Peter on the ship. The Vichy government gave him permission to leave France, and ordered the police to stop threatening him. Several weeks before the ship was due to leave, Madame Cavailhon took Peter by train to Marseille, accompanied by her little girl, whom Peter adored. After a sad goodbye, Peter went to spend the next few weeks at a children's home just outside of Marseille called Les Caillols, run by a kind Belgian couple.

By 1942 many nations had become allies against the Nazis, including the United States, Great Britain, and the Soviet Union. Fighting alongside them were the Free French forces under the leadership of General Charles de Gaulle from his base in London. In November, two weeks before Peter was scheduled to leave France, the Allies invaded North Africa, just across the Mediterranean Sea from Marseille. Immediately, the Nazi army marched into the Southern Zone of France and closed the port of Marseille.

PP. 16-17

The Nazis at the farm were a detachment of Waffen-SS—specially trained Nazis who fought alongside the German army. Peter says that the officers started inviting him to their spaghetti dinners and treating him as a mascot. Then one day he was questioned by the captain, and that's when Peter came up with his dangerous story.

Peter left Marseille for Le Chambon on January 17, 1943. Just five days later, there was a massive roundup in Marseille in which four thousand Jews were arrested and deported to concentration camps. Peter never learned who took his diary, but he speculated that it was probably Daniel Trocmé, the director of the children's home where he lived. He believes that Trocmé was concerned that it might fall into the wrong hands and endanger everyone Peter wrote about, including other refugees and the people who helped to shelter and protect them.

PP. 18–19

Le Chambon-sur-Lignon was the largest of thirteen tiny villages on *La Montagne Protestante*—The Protestant Mountain—a community of Huguenots who had fled to this remote area of south central France hundreds of years before to escape persecution by Catholics. During the Nazi occupation, they offered refuge to anyone in need, especially Jewish children. By the end of the occupation, they had saved the lives of about thirty-five hundred Jews, most of them children. The two Protestant pastors of Le Chambon—André Trocmé and Eduard Theis—along with schoolteacher Roger Darcissac, led the rescue effort. At the risk of their own lives, nearly every family in this small region hid at least one refugee. Peter lived in a children's home called Les Grillons, which was run by Le Mouvement international de la réconciliation. The director, Daniel Trocmé, was Pastor André Trocmé's cousin. Peter told us that he liked living at Les Grillons. It was clean, and the food was more plentiful than in Marseille. He was able to attend school for the first time since his parents' arrest, and he made friends. Although he appreciated how dedicated Daniel Trocmé was to all the children at Les Grillons, he still refused to wear the ugly sandals fashioned from old tires that Trocmé gave the children to wear when their own shoes wore out.

Vichy knew there were Jews hiding in Le Chambon, and the police came frequently to try to find them. They threatened the pastors and others, but not a single inhabitant betrayed the Jews hidden in their midst. Unfortunately, Daniel Trocmé's dedication to the refugee children in his care would prove to be his undoing: When the Gestapo came to arrest young Jewish men living at another home he was responsible for, Daniel stood with his charges and tried to protect them. He was arrested along with eighteen of them, and ultimately perished in the Majdanek concentration camp.

There was a strong French Resistance organization in the region. One of the things they did was to create false identity papers for refugees, so that they could escape detection. Some of these refugees were able to remain in the area throughout the Occupation, while others were led by Resistance members on a perilous journey to safety in Switzerland.

"To a sweetie, Pierrot, from a friend who likes you, Odette."
"To my friend Pierrot, in memory of your friend Antonio."
"To my oldest friend, who always makes me mad!"
These are our translations from the French text on the back of Peter's photos; from the United States Holocaust Memorial Museum archives.

"To my love Rosario, from her admiring Peter."
This is Peter's memory of what he wrote (translated by him into English); from our taped interview with him.

Peter told us that he made notes in his new diary in a sort of code, in case it fell into the wrong hands. He doesn't remember now exactly how his code worked, but says that when he wrote, for example, "We played," he probably meant "We were hiding from Nazis"; and when he wrote "I was bored," he probably meant "I did something for the Maquis." (The Maquis was a network of French Resistance fighters.) In this way he was able to continue his habit of writing everything down in his diary without giving away any dangerous information. When you read his diary entries, these coded entries seem innocent.

PP. 20-21

The French Resistance was made up of ordinary people throughout the country who spied on the Nazis, gathered information, sent messages, created false papers, and did anything else they could to sabotage the enemy, all while continuing to lead normal lives. Others became unofficial soldiers, called the Maquis. They hid in the countryside and used information provided by the Resistance to blow up railway and communication lines used by the Nazis, destroy Nazi-controlled factories, and even execute those who collaborated with the Nazis. British and American spies working behind enemy lines supplied the Maquis with weapons. Peter told us that when the Maquis broke into a factory that manufactured propellers for Nazi airplanes, he went with them and watched them plant explosives to destroy the machinery. When the Nazis began using the schoolyard as a parking lot, Peter and his friends slashed the tires of their trucks or scraped together their sugar rations and poured them into the trucks' gas tanks. The next morning they would watch as those trucks pulled away, knowing that within fifteen minutes, the sugar would gum up the engines and the trucks would stop dead.

Peter told us that the Nazis in Figeac started arresting people in their search for members of the Maquis and the Resistance. In his diary, on May 4, he wrote that he received a letter that said he would be leaving soon. Then a few days later another letter came saying that he would go the following morning at 8:00 am. He threw away all of his school notebooks and packed his backpack and then he was told that he would not be leaving the following morning after all. Peter wrote in his diary, "I was forced to go to class and I managed [without the school notebooks]." Three days later, he wrote, "I hope I go soon because I've had enough. In study hall this evening, we heard machine gun fire." The following day, May 12, he wrote, "The town is inundated with Germans and the Maquis is fighting them." On May 16, he was told that he would be leaving the following morning at 8:00. Once again, it didn't happen, but finally, on May 18, he left for Switzerland.

Peter in Bern, Switzerland, in 1945.

Peter described to us his escape across the border into Switzerland. He also showed us the drawing in his diary depicting the barbed-wire fences and a guardhouse. He remembered a young girl getting confused while crossing, mistaking the Swiss border guard for a Nazi, and screaming that they were going the wrong way. He recalled seeing the guard and knowing that he was not a Nazi soldier, because a Nazi would never hold his gun cradled like a baby, the way this guard had.

Once in Switzerland, Peter could have been sent right back over the border to France, but luckily he was allowed to stay. He showed his true identity papers and gave the name and address of a colleague of his father's in Bern, Switzerland, who would vouch for him. Peter was subjected to days of questioning before he was released. During that time he was held in a refugee camp and treated well. In his diary he mentioned several times how much he liked the camp and how good the food was.

BIBLIOGRAPHY

Bollon, Gérard. Interviewed by D.D.D. and K.G.R. Tape recording. November 12, 2002, and April 5, 2004. Le Chambon-sur-Lignon, France.

_____ . "Contribution à l'histoire du Chambon-sur-Lignon: Le foyer universitaire des Roches et la rafle de 1943." *Cahiers de la Haute-Loire* (1996).

_____ . "La Montagne protestante, terre d'accueil et de résistance pendant la seconde guerre mondiale (1939–1945)." *Les Cahiers du Mézenc*, no. 14 (Juillet 2002).

DeSaix, Deborah Durland and Karen Gray Ruelle. *Hidden on the Mountain: Stories of Children Sheltered from the Nazis in Le Chambon.* New York: Holiday House, 2007.

Feigl, Peter. Interviewed by D.D.D. and K.G.R. Tape recording. May 4, 2003. Palm City, Florida.

_____ . Follow-up phone and e-mail interviews by D.D.D. and K.G.R. June 5, 2009; June 7, 2009; November 10, 2010; November 17, 2010; December 5, 2010; December 8 and 9, 2010; January 23, 2011; November 2016.

_____ . Personal diaries, letters, and documents. (United States Holocaust Memorial Museum archives).

_____ . Oral history. Interviewed by representative of the United States Holocaust Memorial Museum. Transcript of video recording. August 23, 1995.

_____ . Complete working transcript of "One Man, Two Voices: Peter Feigl's Diary and Testimony." Shared by the creators of the educational program, USC Shoah Foundation.

Flaud, Annik. Interviewed by D.D.D. and K.G.R. November 11, 2002. Le Chambon-sur-Lignon, France.

Fogelman, Eva. *Conscience and Courage: Rescuers of Jews During the Holocaust.* New York: Anchor Books/Random House, 1995.

Greenfeld, Howard. *The Hidden Children.* New York: Ticknor & Fields, 1993.

Hacker, Jonathan. *The Hidden Children of France.* UK: Timewatch BBC, 2007. DVD documentary.

Harran, Marilyn et al., *The Holocaust Chronicle: A History in Words and Pictures.* Lincolnwood, Ill.: Publications International, Ltd., 2002.

Henry, Patrick. "Daniel's Choice: Daniel Trocmé (1912–1944)." *The French Review 74*, no. 4 (March 2001).

Lazin, Lauren. *I'm Still Here: Real Diaries of Young People Who Lived During the Holocaust.* MTV Production, 2005. DVD documentary.

Marks, Jane. *The Hidden Children: The Secret Survivors of the Holocaust.* New York: Fawcett Columbine, 1993.

Le Plateau Vivarais-Lignon: Accueil et Resistance 1939–1944: Actes du Colloque du Chambon-sur-Lignon. Le Chambon-sur-Lignon: Societe d'Histoire de la Montagne, 1992.

Rogasky, Barbara. *Smoke and Ashes: The Story of the Holocaust*. Revised and expanded edition. New York: Holiday House, 2002.

Sauvage, Pierre. *Weapons of the Spirit: The Astonishing Story of a Unique Conspiracy of Goodness*. Los Angeles: Chambon Foundation (originally Friends of Le Chambon, Pierre Sauvage Productions, 1989. DVD/VHS documentary.

RECOMMENDED RESOURCES

BOOKS

Two asterisks (**) indicate books recommended for teenagers and adults; one asterisk (*) indicates books for pre-teens to adults; books without asterisks are suitable for children of any age.

*DeSaix, Deborah Durland and Karen Gray Ruelle. *Hidden on the Mountain: Stories of Children Sheltered from the Nazis in Le Chambon*. New York: Holiday House, 2007.

**Gilbert, Martin. *The Routledge Atlas of the Holocaust*. London and New York: Routledge, 2002.

**Hallie, Philip. *Lest Innocent Blood Be Shed: The Story of the Village of Le Chambon and How Goodness Happened There*. New York: Harper Perennial/HarperCollins, 1994.

**Harran, Marilyn et al. *The Holocaust Chronicle: A History in Words and Pictures*. Lincolnwood, Ill.: Publications International, Ltd., 2002.

*Kustanowitz, Esther. *The Hidden Children of the Holocaust: Teens Who Hid from the Nazis*. New York: Rosen Publishing Group, 1999.

*Leapman, Michael. *Witnesses to War: Eight True-Life Stories of Nazi Persecution*. London and New York: Viking/ Penguin, 1998.

Macdonald, Maryann. *Odette's Secrets*. New York: Bloomsbury, 2013.

*Matas, Carol. *Greater Than Angels*. New York: Simon & Schuster Books for Young Readers, 1998.

Millman, Isaac. *Hidden Child*. New York: Farrar, Straus and Giroux, 2005.

*Rogasky, Barbara. *Smoke and Ashes: The Story of the Holocaust*. Revised and expanded edition. New York: Holiday House, 2002.

Steiner, Connie Colker. *Shoes for Amelie*. Montreal: Lobster Press, 2001.

*Zapruder, Alexandra, ed. *Salvaged Pages: Young Writers' Diaries of the Holocaust*. New Haven: Yale University Press, 2002.

EDUCATIONAL PROGRAMS

One Man, Two Voices: Peter Feigl's Diary and Testimony
http://sfi.usc.edu/lessons/one-man-two-voices-peter-feigl's-diary-and-testimony

This educational resource originated by pairing Peter's wartime diary (1942–1944) from Alexandra Zapruder's book *Salvaged Pages* with his USC Shoah Foundation Institute's post-war video testimony (1997) in order to demonstrate how the two primary sources inform each other about Peter's war-time experiences. In addition, by arranging and layering an assortment of other primary sources—including a number of recently discovered and previously unpublished letters, forms, and photos—students encounter a broader perspective and additional context for Peter's experiences. Used in conjunction with one another, these key pieces of historical evidence engage students in historical inquiry and allow them to humanize history through a meaningful, personal connection with Holocaust survivor Peter Feigl.

Sarah's Attic
www.grenierdesarah.org

This site is intended to introduce eight- to-eleven-year-olds to the history of the Holocaust, especially in France. It tells the stories of five Jewish children's experiences during the Holocaust, and includes an exploration of Judaism and European Jewish culture. This program is on the website for France's Memorial de la Shoah (listed below).

FILMS

Au Revoir, les Enfants. Louis Malle. France: PG. Nouvelles Éditions de Films, 1987.

I'm Still Here: Real Diaries of Young People Who Lived During the Holocaust. Lauren Lazin. MTV Production, 2005. DVD documentary.

Le Chambon: La Colline aux Mille Enfants. Jean-Louis Lorenzi. Worcester, Pa.: Gateway Films, 1994.

Weapons of the Spirit: The Astonishing Story of a Unique Conspiracy of Goodness. Pierre Sauvage. Los Angeles: Chambon Foundation (Friends of Le Chambon), Pierre Sauvage Productions, 1989. DVD/VHS documentary.

This important film was re-released in 2019 in a new, remastered 30th-anniversary edition (93 min.). There is also a newly remastered Classroom Version (40 min.). Information is available at www.chambon.org.

WEBSITES

The Chambon Foundation
www.chambon.org

Memorial de la Shoah
www.memorialdelashoah.org/en

USC Shoah Foundation
http://sfi.usc.edu

United States Holocaust Memorial Museum
www.ushmm.org

PHOTO CREDITS

The photographs in this book are from the following sources and are used with permission:

Chambon Foundation (*Weapons of the Spirit*):
   pp. 17 (bottom) and 18

Peter Feigl (private collection): pp. 5, 12, and 23 (left)

The United States Holocaust Memorial Museum (USHMM):
   courtesy of Estelle Bechoefer: p. 6
   courtesy of Peter Feigl: Jacket, pp. 11 (bottom), 19
      (all photos), 21, 23 (right), 24 (all photos), and 34
   courtesy of Jack Lewin: p. 11 (top)
   courtesy of National Archives and Records
      Administration, College Park: pp. 7 (right) and 9
   courtesy of Unknown Provenance: p. 7 (left)
   image courtesy of Peter Feigl: pp. 13 and 17 (top)

ACKNOWLEDGMENTS

It has been a privilege to get to know Peter Feigl and tell his inspiring story. You don't often come across people like Peter, with his moxie in the face of danger coupled with his irrepressible charm. We can't thank him enough for all his support and enthusiasm. We'd also like to thank the librarians and archivists of the United States Holocaust Memorial Museum for their tremendous help.

INDEX

Page numbers in *italics* refer to photographs and illustrations in the text.

Anschluss, 26
anti-Semitism, 5, *7*, 7–8, 25, 28
    see also Holocaust; Nazis
Antwerp, 27
Aryan racism, *7*
Auch, 11, 28, 29
Auschwitz death camp, 22, 25
Austria, *7*, 7–8, *9*, 26

Belgium, 8, 10, 27
Berlin, 5
Bern, 34
Bordeaux, 28
Boy Scouts, 27
Brussels, 10, 27

Cavailhon, Madame, 14–15, 30–31
    see also Condom
concentration camps, 25, 29, 31, 32
Condom, 12–14, 29–30
    see also Cavailhon, Madame
Czechoslovakia, 7, 26

Darcissac, Roger, 32
de Gaulle, Charles, 31
death camps, 22, 25, 29

diaries
    Peter's first diary, *13*, 13–17, *17*, 23, 25, 30, 32
    Peter's second diary, 19–23, *21*, 25, 33
Drancy transit camp, 29–30

Feigl, Lennie, 22, *23*
Feigl, Peter
    childhood (1929–41), 5, *5*, 7–8, 10–12, *11–12*, *24*, 25–29
    in hiding (1942–43), 12–20, *17*, *24*, 29–34
    escape (1944–45), 20–22, *21*, 34, *34*
    in America (1946–), 22–23, *23*
Figeac, 19–20, 34
Final Solution of the Jewish Question, 25
French Resistance, 20, 32–34

Geneva, 21
Gestapo, 16, 18, 32
Gurs internment camp, 10, *11*, 28

Hitler, Adolf, 5, *6*, 7–8, 25–26
Hitler Youth, 26
Holland, 10, 27
Holocaust, 25
Holocaust Memorial Museum, U.S., 23, 25
Huguenots, 32